Today's Encouraging Word

60 Seconds of Inspiration to Start Your Day

karl eastlack

Today's Encouraging Word

60 Seconds of Inspiration to Start Your Day

—— karl eastlack ——

wesleyan
publishing
house

Indianapolis, Indiana

Contents

On Christ, the Solid Rock,

I stand.

All other ground is sinking sand.

—Edward Mote

Balance

Something unique occurred when a patient was visiting her doctor. The two were seated across from each other at a mahogany desk located in front of a picture window overlooking a beautiful courtyard.

During the consultation, the physician leaned back leisurely on his swivel chair but soon realized that he was out of balance. His momentum propelled him backwards as his hands began to flail in the air, searching for anything secure. In a final act of desperation, he grabbed the venetian blinds with both hands and narrowly avoided landing on the floor.

Balance is crucial not only with swivel chairs but also in life. When God is not at the center of our lives, we discover that life is out of balance and nothing seems to go right.

The Bible tells us that when we seek the kingdom of God and His righteousness (Matt. 6:33), all of the other parts of our lives begin to make sense. God is the secure footing that you have been searching for.

Live It!

Read Matthew, chapter 6, and ask yourself, "Does my life reflect Christ's description of a balanced life?" Choose one thing you can do today to bring some balance to your life.

Let another praise you, and not

your own mouth;

someone else,

and not your own lips.

—Proverbs 27:2

AUTHENTICITY

A group of college students gathered to hear a panel of business owners share their secrets of success. Each speaker gave a brief history of his or her career as well as some practical advice for the students. The students, however, began to feel discouraged because the success stories seemed to be so far beyond their ability.

But when it was time for one of the more prominent business people to speak, he began by saying, "I want to share with you twelve things that you should never do in business." He then went on to explain twelve major mistakes he had made over his many years in business. The list included simple yet costly mistakes that he had made in judgment and timing as well as the lesson that he had learned from each one. The students were delighted.

The Bible says that God exalts those who humble themselves. By being honest about himself, this businessman made it possible for others to benefit from his experience. Honesty remains the best policy with God, my friend.

Live It!

The next time you are asked to showcase your successes, have the freedom to tell the "whole story."

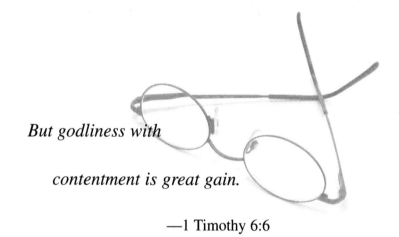

But godliness with

contentment is great gain.

—1 Timothy 6:6

CONTENTMENT

Consider these famous words of William Shakespeare: "Striving to be better, we often mar what's well." Ponder John the Baptist's challenge: "Be content with your pay" (Luke 3:14). Reflect on this confession by the Apostle Paul: "I have learned the secret of being content in any and every situation, whether well fed or hungry . . ." (Phil. 4:12).

Contentment is a lost art today. We seem to be never satisfied.

Be warned, however, if you become a content person, you will always be outnumbered and outvoted. It isn't enjoyable to march out of step with others. But, if you choose to be content, a new dimension of your character will take shape and you'll be a free person indeed. Satisfied. Contented. Those wonderful, old-fashioned words make for excellent living in today's world!

Live It!

Write down as many personal blessings as you can in two minutes. Now read your list out loud and let that wonderful feeling of contentment arise within you. It feels good, doesn't it?

I know, my God, that you test the

heart and are pleased with integrity.

—1 Chronicles 29:17

HONESTY

Due to the loss of an eye during the second World War, Israeli statesman Moshe Dyan had to wear an eye patch. One day, Dyan was stopped for speeding, and he quipped to the policeman, "Look, I have only one eye. Which do you want me to watch, the speedometer or the road?"

That funny but true story tells us much about human nature. We hate having to face the music concerning our wrong words or actions. We would rather fudge the truth a bit or find the loopholes in the rules. But I think that we can do better than that.

God's Holy Bible challenges us to be honest and truthful even when it might lead us to discipline or punishment. This is true whether you are a child or an adult, a truck driver or the president of a country. So shoot a straight arrow. Be known as a person of integrity, and don't be afraid to take responsibility for your actions. As my godly mother often said, "Honesty is still the best policy."

Live It!

Have you been less than honest lately? Have you cut some corners at work? Bow your head before God and have an honest talk with your merciful, loving Father.

Breathe on me, breath of God;

Fill me with life anew,

That I may love what Thou dost love,

And do what Thou wouldst do.

—Edwin Hatch

Priorities

Here is a wise saying from Stephen Covey: "Anything less than a conscious commitment to the important is an unconscious commitment to the unimportant." Before you go on, please read that quote again.

It is easy to let the hard knocks of life dictate what I do and with whom I do it. For example: My work comes at me a thousand miles per hour, dictating the use of my time. If I'm not careful to choose otherwise, that business could drift over into other very important areas such as family time. If I don't choose to commit to my family, I am really choosing to deny them their father and husband, making subtle statements to them about what is really important to me.

God's Holy Bible calls us to remember the truly important things in life. Jesus Christ said, "What good is it for a man to gain the whole world, and yet lose or forfeit his very self?" (Luke 9:25). That might well be asked of our culture today.

Live It!

List the most important people and activities in your life. Do you need to reshape your time commitment to them? If so, be bold, and do something about it.

I pray also that the eyes of your

heart may be enlightened in

order that you may know the hope

to which he has called you, the

riches of his glorious inheritance

in the saints.

—Ephesians 1:18

LIFE

How old are you? You can tell me. I won't spill the beans.

Mark Twain said, "Life would be infinitely happier if we could only be born at eighty and gradually approach eighteen!" Have you ever thought that too?

Life is a mixture of headaches, heartaches, thrills, peace and quiet, deafening noise, happy memories, great relationships, irritating people all rolled together until the grim reaper finally catches up with us.

In God's Holy Bible, Jesus Christ says, "I have come that they may have life, and have it to the full" (John 10:10). That sounds promising, doesn't it?

Has life got you hog-tied and frustrated? Have you been looking for a way out of your tough situation only to find that someone has put bars on all the windows and doors? Why not turn it over to Jesus Christ today? His promise of abundant life is yours for the asking.

Live It!

Meditate on the ways in which God has cared for you in the past. Create an atmosphere of gratitude to surround your current tough situation. Then, relax and live life to the full.

And why do you worry about

clothes? See how the lilies of

the field grow. They do not labor

or spin. Yet I tell you that not

even Solomon in all his splendor

was dressed like one of these.

—Matthew 6:28–29

TRUST

Worry is one of the common emotions that unite all of humanity. We are worrywarts! If there's nothing to worry about, we create something, because, well, that's what we do best.

Charlie Brown once said, "I've developed a new philosophy. I only dread one day at a time." Actually, good ol' Charlie is not far off from the best way to handle the things that worry us. The best philosopher of all time, Jesus Christ said, "Do not worry about tomorrow, for tomorrow will worry about itself. Each day has enough trouble of its own" (Matt. 6:34). Jesus' guiding principle is "Live one day at a time."

While this is great advice, most of us either let the past haunt us or let the future give us ulcers and panic attacks. Yet Jesus Christ desires health for us. There really is no need to tie ourselves up into emotional knots, and we won't do it if we'll follow His advice. Turn all your dilemmas and problems over to the One who really cares, then learn to live one day at a time.

Live It!

Do not think about what you need to do tomorrow. Spend today only on today.

Each of you should look not only

to your own interests, but also

to the interests of others. Your

attitude should be the same as

that of Christ Jesus. . . .

—Philippians 2:4–5

KINDNESS

We live in a highly materialistic and selfish age. We work hard for what we have, and we like to keep it for ourselves. We typically move through each day giving little thought to the people around us. When we get right down to it, we generally live for ourselves. Do you agree?

Mother Teresa once said, "Unless life is lived for others, it is not worthwhile."

You see, what makes us human is our capacity to live beyond our own needs, to see how we might be able to enhance someone else's life.

Little things really can make a difference. Why not get a cup of coffee for someone else when you pour a cup for yourself? Why not make a donation to a local charity or give blood today? Every time you benefit someone else by what you do, you are rising to your highest potential as a human being.

God's Holy Bible tells us to love others as we have been loved by God. Don't bottle kindness up. Give it away, my friend. You will make the world a better place.

Live It!

Find someone who seems a bit down and bless him or her with a word of encouragement. Go ahead, make their day!

Do not be anxious about anything,

but in everything, by prayer and

petition, with thanksgiving,

present your requests to God.

—Philippians 4:6

Control

Every pilot knows the value of communicating with the control tower, especially during times of crisis or trouble. The natural reaction of a pilot is to radio for help. Yet we don't always do this in our own daily living, do we? Why is that?

Often our tendency is to try and make it on our own. Like Frank Sinatra, we do it our way.

God's Holy Bible sings another song. It says, "I (Jesus) am the vine; you are the branches. If a man remains in me and I in him, he will bear much fruit; apart from me you can do nothing" (John 15:5).

While I was recently contemplating those words, God began to deal with me. I thought I could handle things that were less than a crisis without His help. But I have learned that, whether in calm or rough times, blue skies or dark, I must keep in contact with my control tower, God Himself. I hope you will do the same, my friend. He's waiting to hear from you today. Roger?

Live It!

Find three "small" needs to bring to your Father today. Fight the thought that God is interested only in the big things. Let God sweat the small stuff with you.

Finally, brothers, whatever is true,

whatever is noble, whatever is

right, whatever is pure, whatever

is lovely, whatever is admirable—if

anything is excellent or praiseworthy—

think about such things.

—Philippians 4:8

LOVE

Everybody has been wounded by someone else at least once. Folks can be so cruel sometimes, can't they? When that happens, we often become bitter, even hateful, toward the person who has wronged us.

The problem with hatred is that usually we end up hurting ourselves. One person wrote, "Hating people is like burning down your house to get rid of a rat." Hatred feeds the forces of bigotry, cynicism, and division. It consumes our thoughts as we dwell on ways to get even. Revenge is an empty cup; it never delivers what it promises.

In His Word, God tells us to love one another as He has loved us (John 13:34). That seems like a pretty difficult command to follow, unless the One who commanded it lives in you.

Live It!

Turn your anger over to God. He will free you of anything that produces hatred and bitterness, if you'll let Him.

Get rid of all bitterness, rage and

anger, brawling and slander, along

with every form of malice.

—Ephesians 4:31

RECONCILIATION

Are you angry with someone today? I mean, absolutely furious? Aristotle wrote, "Anyone can become angry—that is easy. But to be angry with the right person, to the right degree, at the right time, for the right purpose, and in the right way, now that is not easy!"

I agree, don't you?

God's Holy Bible tells us to not let the sun go down on our anger (Eph. 4:26). That suggests some important principles to follow:

Settle relationship accounts today. Don't put them off.

Allow yourself to feel appropriate anger, but remember that anger usually has more to do with you than with the other person.

Don't stay angry. Pride keeps us away from people, leaving us disconnected and disappointed.

God's way is to heal broken relationships, helping people get rid of those ugly emotions that churn stomachs and haunt heads. Why not try His way today?

Live It!

Write a note or an e-mail to the person with whom you are angry to begin the process of restoration. Someone has to make the first move. Why not you?

No one can make you again but he

who made you the first time.

—Webster Fullerton

CHANGE

Most people would change something about themselves if they could. It might be something small like a bad attitude or losing a few pounds, or it might be something big like overcoming a drug habit or a drinking problem.

As a casual observer of people, I am intrigued by the ways in which we try to change ourselves. We buy books, take courses on change management, and even make New Year's resolutions. Try them all, if you wish.

Yet I might suggest giving God a try. After all, He's the One who designed and made you. The psalmist says that we were knit by God in our mother's womb (Ps. 139:13). He who made us is the One who is able to remake us, if we are willing to trust Him with that remaking.

Trust God with the changes you need to make. He'll do a better job than anyone else. He loves you and wants to produce the best in you. He really does.

Live It!

Don't take too big a bite today. Find just one area you need to change and take it to God.

But because you say so, I will let

down the nets.

—The Apostle Peter (Luke 5:5)

FAITH

There was once a preacher who spoke about the relationship between fact and faith. He said, "That you are sitting here before me in this church is a fact. That I am standing here, speaking to you from this pulpit is a fact. That I believe anyone is actually listening to me is pure faith."

What is faith? It is the belief that God knows what He is doing, even when we don't fully understand. In fact, God's Holy Bible tells us that "faith is being sure of what we hope for and certain of what we do not see" (Heb. 11:1). I have come to believe that God does know what He is doing. In fact, He has a great track record in my life. Personal experience has taught me that I can trust God with my life and my future.

We all put our faith in something or someone. What do you trust? The stock market? Your health? Your family? Planet earth? Every one of those things will one day be gone, yet God will still be bringing His good life to you.

Why not put your faith in God? You won't be disappointed, and that's a fact!

Live It!

Is there something that you need to trust God for, even if you don't quite understand the path He is taking? Do it. Trust Him today.

All Scripture is God-breathed and

is useful for teaching, rebuking,

correcting and training in

righteousness. . . .

—2 Timothy 3:16

SCRIPTURE

I read an interesting statistic recently: the average American home has three Bibles in it. Three Bibles! Yet we are the most biblically illiterate generation of Americans to have ever lived.

Why is that? Perhaps it is because we so rarely pick up one of the three Bibles that we own. We seldom read God's Word to find out how to live in today's complicated world. That's too bad because we need the truth now more than ever!

President Woodrow Wilson once said, "When you have read the Bible, you will know it is the word of God because you will have found it to be the key to your heart, your own happiness, and your own way of living."

There are many things that you could choose to do with your time, such as watching movies or reading the newspaper. These are valid things to do. But if you wish to enhance your life and your family, read God's Holy Bible. It is a lost treasure for these days. Why not take some time soon to rediscover that treasure for you and your family?

Live It!

Go ahead and pick up a Bible! If it's been a while, begin by reading the Gospel of John. It'll be like visiting an old friend!

But I have raised you up for this

very purpose, that I might show you my

power and that my name

might be proclaimed in all the earth.

—Exodus 9:16

DESTINY

Have you ever heard the following quote? "I expect to pass through this world once. Any good, therefore, that I can do, or any kindness that I can show to a fellow creature, let me do it now. Let me not defer or neglect it, for I shall not pass this way again."

Why were you born? Have you ever asked yourself that important question? This earth was meant to be a better place because of your presence. If you are merely a taker in this life, always taking from others without giving back, you are robbing the world of your gift, the reason for which you were born.

Is your neighborhood a better place because you live there? How about your workplace? Is your spouse a better person having been married to you? What about your kids? Are they better people because you're their parent?

Live life to the fullest, my friend. Be a giver and not a taker. There's no better way to enjoy the ride.

Live It!

Ask a trusted friend or family member to tell you what they see in you. See if you agree. Then, take pleasure in living today as God's precious gift to this weary world.

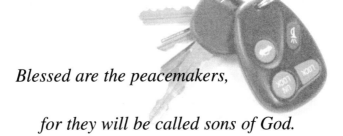

Blessed are the peacemakers,

for they will be called sons of God.

—Matthew 5:9

Harmony

I read a magazine article that described how neighbors often get angry with each other, allowing small problems to escalate into "World War III." Has that ever happened to you?

God's Holy Bible tells us that it is hard to stop a quarrel once it begins. Have you found that to be true? Isn't it amazing how something small can grow into something that devastates relationships? Or two families? Or two nations?

The philosopher Seneca wrote that there is no battle unless there be two. God's Bible tells us that, as much as it is possible, we are to live at peace with each other. You can never determine the actions and reactions of the other person, but you always have full control over yourself. Choose to live in harmony with others.

Live It!

Why not settle that long-running quarrel today? Extend the hand of friendship to your enemy, offering peace where there once was strife. Your world will be a better place.

When I smiled at them, they

scarcely believed it;

the light of my face was precious

to them.

—Job 29:24

SMILES

Did you know that it takes seventy-two muscles to frown and only fourteen to smile? A smile costs nothing, but gives much. It enriches those who receive without making poorer those who give it. It takes but a moment, but the memory of it sometimes lasts forever.

None are so rich or mighty that they can get along without a smile, and none are so poor that they cannot be made rich by it. A smile creates happiness in the home, fosters goodwill in business, and is the countersign of friendship. It brings rest to the weary, cheer to the discouraged, sunshine to the sad, and is nature's best antidote for trouble.

Yet a smile cannot be bought, begged, borrowed, or stolen. It has no value to anyone until it is given away.

Some people are too tired to give you a smile. So give them one of yours, as no one needs a smile so much as he who has none to give.

Live It!

Find at least three people who could use a smile, and give them one of yours. Be creative, and have fun!

Keep me from my deceitful ways;

be gracious to me through your law.

I have chosen the way of truth;

I have set my heart on your laws.

—Psalm 119:29–30

TRUTHFULNESS

I heard of a woman, apparently pregnant, who walked out of the grocery store without buying anything. The assistant manager became suspicious and stopped her, whereupon she "gave birth" to a pound of butter, a chuck roast, a bottle of pancake syrup, two tubes of toothpaste, and several bars of candy!

It is estimated that more then three billion dollars is lost annually through shoplifting.

Frankly, I think truthfulness is one of the most appealing aspects of Christianity. Christ does not offer a technique for rebuilding your life. He offers you His life, His honesty, His integrity. These are not rules and laws, but an inner power that counteracts our dishonest bent. God's Holy Bible calls this a "new nature" (2 Cor. 5:17).

Receiving God's power is not just the best way to stop being dishonest, it is the *only* way. Entrust your nature to Jesus Christ. You, and everyone around you, will win.

Live It!

Is there something that you have been dishonest about? Why not correct it before another day goes by. Ask God for strength and help.

A man who lacks judgment derides

his neighbor,

but a man of understanding holds

his tongue.

—Proverbs 11:12

KINDNESS

Have you ever been around a sarcastic person? Do you tend to be one?

Someone once said that sarcasm is jealousy in bold disguise. I believe it. The times that I have allowed myself to be sarcastic have been the times that, deep in my heart, I was jealous of something about another person.

When we are jealous of someone, we try to tear that person down to make him or her look bad in some way.

God's Holy Bible has much to say about the way we treat others. To the jealous person, God says, "Do not covet" (Ex. 20:17). Being envious divides people from each other. It makes us suspicious and negative.

God, on the other hand, is interested in uniting people. He looks for people who want to show the best side of humanity, not the worst.

So be careful of your sarcasm. It may mean that there is jealousy lurking just under the surface of your heart. Take it to God and let Him soften your attitude. He's good at that.

Live It!

If you have a tendency to speak negatively about a particular person, ask God to help you stop it. Try to find something nice to say about that person.

A generous man will prosper;

he who refreshes others will

himself be refreshed.

—Proverbs 11:25

GENEROSITY

Our world seems to be full of takers, people who never sacrifice themselves or are generous with others. Being a giver, on the other hand, is a very rewarding lifestyle. It is contagious also. When we are generous, we not only feel the wind at our backs, those around us do as well.

Listen to a verse from God's Word: "Each man should give what he has decided in his heart to give, not reluctantly or under compulsion, for God loves a cheerful giver" (2 Cor. 9:7).

When Jesus challenged His followers to be unselfish, He taught that it is "more blessed to give than to receive" (Acts 20:35). He connected living a good life with being a giving person. The fact is, you get blessed each time you bless someone else. What a great way to live!

Live It!

At least once today, go out of your way to be generous. Take some fruit or snacks to people at work. While in line at the store, let the person behind you go first. Watch the ripple effect that your generosity has on others.

A generous man will prosper;

he who refreshes others will

himself be refreshed.

—Proverbs 11:25

PEACEMAKING

Have you known someone that you really hated to be around? Someone who seemed to be against everything you did or said? Someone who became your enemy?

God's Holy Bible says something interesting about our attitude toward our enemies: "You have heard that it was said, 'Love your neighbor and hate your enemy. But I tell you: Love your enemies and pray for those who persecute you . . . " (Matt. 5:43–44).

Enemies are difficult to deal with. They get under our skin like no one else. But there is a way out of that predicament, if you choose to take it. Abraham Lincoln recognized that when he wrote, "The best way to destroy your enemy is to make him your friend." Now, there's a different approach!

Why not try this new way of dealing with an enemy? Be kind to him or her, and see what happens. That person might not change, but you'll sleep better knowing that you took the high road.

Live It!

Approach one of the difficult people in your life with a kind word. Speak it, write it, e-mail it, whatever. Try to make your enemy your friend.

A happy heart makes the

face cheerful.

—Proverbs 15:13

TODAY

An American poet wrote, "Since life is short we need to make it broad. Since life is brief, we need to make it bright."

It's true, isn't it? While we have little control over the length of our life, we do have some control over each day in which we live.

God's Holy Bible tells us to "number our days" (Ps. 90:12), carefully making the most of each day. How do we make life broad, as the poet suggested? By filling it with friends and activities that build us up, making us better people along the way.

How do we make life bright? Some would say that if we make enough money or buy the right things, then our life will be bright. I beg to differ. I believe that when we bring a smile to someone else's face, or make someone else's day a little more pleasant, when we decide that we're going to focus on what is good rather than on problems, we experience bright days.

We have been given a gift called today. Enjoy it!

Live It!

Walk more slowly throughout the day. Plan to notice things that you usually breeze by. Enjoy all the moments of this day.

A cheerful look brings joy to

    the heart,

and good news gives health to the

    bones.

—Proverbs 15:30

ATTITUDE

Sydney Harris wrote, "When I hear somebody sigh that 'Life is hard,' I am always tempted to ask, 'compared to what?'"

The longer I live, the more I am convinced that our happiness or unhappiness depends more on our attitude toward the events of life than on the events themselves.

Even God's Holy Bible points to that fact. It says, "When a man is gloomy, everything seems to go wrong. When he is cheerful, everything seems right." Isn't that the truth? Comedian Flip Wilson got it right when he said, "What you see is what you get."

How is your outlook today? Notice I didn't ask "How are your circumstances today?" Life will throw all kinds of situations in your path. How you see them will determine how they affect you.

So determine to think good, positive thoughts today, thoughts that encourage you as well as those around you. As Helen Keller put it, "Keep your face to the sunshine and you will not be able to see the shadow."

Live It!

If something unpleasant comes your way today, look for a blessing hidden within the difficulty. You'll enjoy the results.

Commit to the Lord whatever you do,

and your plans will succeed.

—Proverbs 16:3

PROCRASTINATION

Procrastination is my sin.

It brings me naught but sorrow.

I know that I should stop it.

In fact, I will—tomorrow!

—Author Unknown

I have learned from previous experience that the best way to make something seem hard, is to keep putting it off. Sometimes the things we procrastinate are small, insignificant things, such as washing the car or mowing the lawn. But to be honest, we'd have to admit that some major items get left undone also. Things like—

Saying "I love you"

Writing a thank-you letter

Calling our mothers

Calling on God

That last item is one that many people put off until the very last moment. God's Word tells us that if you search for God in earnest, you will find Him (Deut. 4:29). Why not search for God today? He's there, and He loves you.

Live It!

Do one thing from the list above.

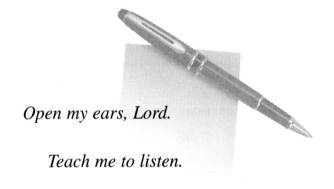

Open my ears, Lord.

Teach me to listen.

—Bob Cull

LISTENING

Poet Edward H. Richards wrote: "A wise old owl sat on an oak. The more he saw, the less he spoke. The less he spoke, the more he heard. Why aren't we like that wise old bird?"

God's Holy Bible gives similar advice in the book of James. "Everyone should be quick to listen, slow to speak and slow to become angry . . ." (1:19). Those are good words to live by, don't you think?

My mom used to say that God gave me two beautiful ears but only one mouth because He expects me to listen twice as much as I speak. Do you know how hard that is for an opinionated person like me? I am learning to reel in the excesses of my personality, and I've found that we can learn a lot just by being good listeners. In fact, there are too many talkers in our world and not enough listeners.

I propose that we make better use of our two beautiful ears today. Are you listening? I hope so. Now it's my turn to get quiet.

Live It!

Today, practice the discipline of listening. Be careful not to talk over others. Count to five before responding to anything.

He who pursues righteousness and

love finds life, prosperity and

honor.

—Proverbs 21:21

CHARACTER

It takes years of hard work to develop character within us. All kinds of trials come along to test and to develop our character. Those years of investment finally pay off as integrity and character finally take root in our lives.

Then along comes a temptation that appeals to our dark side, something that would quickly destroy our character. Our first reaction might be to think that no one will ever find out, that it will hurt no one.

But God's Holy Bible says that we can be certain of one thing: our sin will be exposed. What is done in secret will someday be brought to light.

Don't be fooled, my friend, by the momentary appeal of temptation. It will leave a sour taste for years to come, not only to you but also to your loved ones. Don't be overwhelmed by temptation. You can be a person of integrity. You can stand up to temptation and walk away from it, with God's help. You don't need to give in.

Live It!

If you are flirting around the edges of a temptation, walk away today. Ask God to help you let it go. Then thank God for giving you the strength to live with integrity.

When I was a boy of fourteen, my

father was so ignorant I could hardly stand

to have the old man around. But when I got

to be twenty one, I was astonished at how

much the old man had learned!

—Mark Twain

PRIVILEGE

Someone wrote, "He can climb the highest mountain, or swim the biggest ocean. He can fly the fastest plane, and fight the strongest tiger. But most of the time he just carries out the garbage. He's my father."

Being a dad is a hard job. Some of the most important memories that shape our lives today were created by interacting with or watching our fathers. Wow! That's a real burden for us dads to carry. Being a dad is a tough job, but it's one that we want, and we really do want to be the best dads we can be. We don't always get it right, but we keep trying. We want to do our best for our kids' sake. Someday they'll thank us for being their dad. In the meantime we want them to know that we are grateful for the privilege of being their fathers. Imperfect? Yes! But we love our children, and that's what matters most.

Live It!

If your dad is still alive, write a note of gratitude to him. If you are a dad, tell your kids how much you love them.

The Lord is my light and my salvation—

whom shall I fear?

The Lord is the stronghold of my life—

of whom shall I be afraid?

—Psalm 27:1

CALM

I like what someone once wrote about faith: "Fear knocked on the door. Faith answered. No one was there!"

When I was little, I had many fears: someone was under my bed at night, monsters were in the basement, ghosts were making creaky noises. I was a real scaredy-cat.

As I grew up, my fears changed, but fear was still there. I had financial fears, relationship fears, fears about physical health, popularity fears. Then one day I came across a verse from God's Holy Bible that says, "Perfect love drives out fear" (1 John 4:18).

I realized that I was spending too much time focusing on the things that made me afraid rather than thinking of the things that calm me. Now, God's love makes me more relaxed, more confident. The Bible also tells us that if God is for us, no one can stand against us. His love in my life allows me to stand and not faint when fears show up.

God loves you today, my friend. Relax. Fear not, for He is with you wherever you go.

Live It!

Face a fear today. Stand up to it knowing that God loves you. Tell someone else about your adventure, and ask him or her to pray for you as you face your fear.

You have heard that it was said,

"Eye for eye, and tooth for tooth."

But I tell you, Do not resist an evil

person. If someone strikes you on

the right cheek, turn to him the

other also. And if someone wants

to sue you and take your tunic, let

him have your cloak as well.

—Matthew 5:38–40

ACCEPTANCE

I've heard it said that people who fight fire with fire usually end up with ashes. There is a lot of truth in that statement.

Is there someone in your life right now who is driving you crazy? Perhaps someone has been quite irritating lately? Maybe someone has been attacking you unmercifully. How should you respond?

God's Word gives us a precious bit of advice called the Golden Rule: "Do to others what you would have them do to you . . ." (Matt. 7:12). This "rule" really frees people. It won't stop the perpetrator from bothering you, but it will free your heart from the anxiety of dealing with the negative relationship.

You have a choice. You can fight back, returning evil for evil, or you can do something that brings peace between the two of you. Take the higher road; follow the Golden Rule. You'll be glad you did.

Live It!

Do something nice for an irritating person. Give a cup of coffee, hold open a door, or write a nice note. You won't believe the results.

But those who hope in the Lord

will renew their strength.

They will soar on wings like eagles;

they will run and not grow weary,

they will walk and not be faint.

—Isaiah 40:31

STRENGTH

There are times when life becomes difficult and we feel like quitting. Everything presses in around us, and our future looks bleak. Instead of facing each day with excitement and expectation, we face it with weariness, even depression. Some people who come up against those times turn to alcohol or drugs for relief, only to find emptiness and disappointment instead.

In life's most difficult hours, remember God's promise: those who hope in Him will renew their strength. Friend, there really is no reason to quit. Please consider what God says in His Holy Bible. Wait before the Lord; let Him quiet your anxious heart. Exchange your weakness for His strength. You'll be amazed at how you soar instead of faint!

Live It!

Instead of quitting your job, marriage, friendship, or even your life, turn to God. Ask Him to lift you up right now.

I know your deeds. See, I have

placed before you an open door

that no one can shut. I know

that you have little strength, yet

you have kept my word and have

not denied my name.

—Revelation 3:8

OPPORTUNITY

Does it seem like you're up against a wall, a closed door? No matter how hard you try to open it, it's definitely closed. Boarded up. Not budging at all.

We run into closed doors all the time. A career path comes to a dead end. A promising relationship doesn't pan out. A health problem seems overwhelming and scary. A financial struggle won't go away. Things like these hang over us constantly, at times even threatening our sanity.

But try looking around. There may be another way to go. Alexander Graham Bell wrote, "When one door closes, another opens; But we often look so long and regretfully upon the closed door that we do not see the one which has opened for us." You'll never know what's out there until you look. An open door just might be around the corner. Go ahead and peek. It's worth a look, isn't it?

Live It!

Stop looking at the closed door. You've studied it long enough. Begin looking for the open door. Hurry, time's wasting!

A word aptly spoken is like apples

of gold in settings of silver.

—Proverbs 25:11

CAUTION

Do you remember the childhood saying "Sticks and stones will break my bones, but words will never hurt me"?

We used to say that in order to let bullies know they were not going to get under our skin. In reality, name-calling really hurt down inside.

Someone said that we should handle words carefully because they have more power than atom bombs. It's true!

God's Holy Bible is the greatest book for showing us how to live a balanced life. It says, "Be quick to listen and slow to speak" (Jas. 1:19). When we speak quickly, we speak dangerously, possible hurting other people along the way. Words can be painful when spoken in anger or jealousy or fear. Choose them carefully.

Live It!

Today, slow down before you respond. Be careful of what you say. Choose your words wisely and lovingly.

Trust and obey,

For there's no other way

To be happy in Jesus,

But to trust and obey.

—James Sammis

DIRECTION

Is it possible to know God's will? Certainly He guided people like Moses, David, and the Apostle Paul, but does He still direct our lives today? God's Word says that He does. "Trust in the LORD with all your heart and lean not on your own understanding; in all your ways acknowledge him, and he will make your paths straight" (Prov. 3:5–6).

These days, we really need God's direction for our families and ourselves, don't we? These are difficult times, but, there are some things we can do to find God's direction:

Trust in the Lord (have faith).

Don't lean on your own understanding (be humble).

Acknowledge God in everything (obey).

God does have a blueprint for our lives, but He needs our cooperation. The formula is simple: trust and obey. We can never be more content with our lives than if they are directed by God himself.

Live It!

Say yes to God in an area of your life where you've been less than obedient. Cross the line right now; choose God's will.

The righteous cry out, and the

Lord hears them;

he delivers them from all their

troubles.

—Psalm 34:17

PROBLEMS

An old preacher once said, "I've got problems, you've got problems. All God's children got problems." Isn't that true? Welcome to the human race!

The issue, then, is not whether we'll have problems, but how we'll handle them.

Harriet Beecher Stowe wrote, "When you get into a tight place and everything goes against you, until it seems as though you cannot hang on a minute longer, never give up, for that is just the place and time that the tide will turn."

Great advice, isn't it? I think many of us give up too quickly when the solution to our problem was right there, ready to be discovered and enjoyed.

God's Word tells us that we can do all things through Christ who gives us strength (Phil. 4:13). It's not our own strength, mind you. It's His strength, which is ours for the asking.

Live It!

If you're up against something that tempts you to give up, turn to Jesus Christ instead. Allow His strength to give you the gumption to keep going.

You need to persevere so that

when you have done the will of

God, you will receive what he has

promised.

—Hebrews 10:36

PERSEVERANCE

A little boy and his sister were climbing up a mountain path when the little sister complained, "This isn't a path at all! It's all bumpy and rocky!" The brother replied, "Sure, but the bumps are what you climb on!"

Most of us respond in predictable ways to the rocks that line the path of our lives. We complain about them, we kick against them, and we hurt ourselves in the process. We try to pick them up and get rid of them, only to discover that they are too heavy for us. A few people give up climbing altogether.

The trouble is that we are accustomed to paved roads and level sidewalks. But life is not made that way. So what shall we do when we encounter problems? Shall we complain? Shall we quit?

God's Holy Bible encourages us to keep going by using life's bumps as stepping-stones. The Bible says, "I can do all things through him who gives me strength" (Phil. 4:13). Trust your life to Jesus Christ and you will find that even the bumps become steps to successful living.

Live It!

Identify one area of your life that is difficult right now. Repeat Phil. 4:13 each time you are reminded of your problem.

Then they cried to the Lord in

their trouble,

and he saved them from their distress.

He sent forth his word and healed

them. . . .

—Psalm 107:19–20

WHOLENESS

One day Jesus visited a place in Jerusalem called Bethesda, which means "house of grace." There were many sick people there, gathered around a pool of water that they believed could heal them. They believed that when the waters were stirred, the first person to get into the pool would be healed.

At Bethesda, Jesus came upon a man that had been crippled for thirty-eight years. He had spent his life sitting by that pool. Jesus asked him, "Do you want to be made well?"

That seems like an obvious question, but did he really want healing?

Sometimes we become comfortable with our problems and nervous about what life would be like without them. Our fears may become excuses for not growing, and our problems may bring us attention and pity.

Jesus asks the same question of us today: Do you want to be made well? Trust God to bring you to a place of deliverance, freedom, and wholeness. He loves you, and He cares.

Live It!

Is there something that you are hanging onto for all the wrong reasons? Give it to God right now, and let him make you well.

I thought, "Age should speak;

advanced years should teach wisdom."

—Job 32:7

RESPECT

What do you think of when you see an elderly person? Are your thoughts mostly negative, such as "Look at that frail person," "That older person shouldn't be driving!" "I'm glad that's not me"?

We make these comments more often than we'd like to admit. We tend to disrespect people of age. Yet there was a time when the elderly were honored people in our society. Their wisdom and experience offered much to the younger generation.

Ramsey Clark wrote, "People who don't cherish their elderly have forgotten whence they came and whither they go." I love to sit and listen to senior adults tell about their past and what they have learned from their many years on earth. Older people have much to give the rest of us. Why not listen, learn, and give respect? You'll put a smile on the face of an honored senior, and maybe even on your own.

Live It!

Go out of your way to honor an elderly person today. Go one step further and encourage another person to do the same. Double the blessing!

A gossip separates close friends.

—Proverbs 16:28

EXCELLENCE

I am always amazed at how relevant God's Holy Bible is for today. For example, recently I read the following verse: "A perverse man stirs up dissension, and a gossip separates close friends" (Prov. 16:28).

Isn't that true? Human beings are sometimes tempted to tell a juicy story about someone else, a story that might or might not be completely true.

One of the many reasons I love God and follow His teaching for my life is that He always tries to bring out the best in me. He wants me to build others up, not tear them down with hurtful words or gossip. God is pro-life in every sense of the word!

Henry Ford said, "My best friend is the one who brings out the best in me." That's God in my life. He always brings out the best.

Today, live in the best way possible. Refuse to tear anyone down with hurtful words. Expect the best from yourself. God does, and He can help you produce it if you'll ask Him.

Live It!

Each time you speak about someone else today, pause and ask yourself: Is it true? Is it necessary? Is it kind?

Jesus declared, "Go now and

leave your life of sin."

—John 8:11

HONESTY

I once read an article which stated that more than half of all married men have cheated on their wives. The article also said that more than half of all students surveyed had cheated on exams, and that more than half of all employees occasionally steal from their company. Someone has said "Forbidden fruit is responsible for many a bad jam." Do you know the meaning of that statement? Something that looks good at first but is wrong to do will always come back to haunt us in the long run. A moment's thrill can easily become a lifetime's pain, not just for us, but for the ones we love.

If you are currently tasting some forbidden fruit, I have a good word for you: Stop, drop, and roll. Stop doing what you know to be wrong. Drop your plans to continue doing it. And roll those energies into the things and people that produce health and peace in your life

Live It!

While reading today's encouraging word, did you think of something you are doing that should be stopped? Stop it today.

Jesus answered, "I am the way and the truth and the life. No one comes to the Father except through me."

—John 14:6

HEAVEN

Have you ever stared into the night sky, wondering what is beyond the stars? Heaven, maybe? I hope so, don't you?

But how does someone get into heaven? God's Holy Bible says that we enter heaven because of God's grace, not because of the good things we've done. If we got there based on good behavior, we could say, "Wow! Look what I've done." Instead, we will be saying, "Wow! Look what God has done for me!"

Mark Twain said, "Heaven comes to us by grace. If it came by merit, you would stay out and your dog would get to go in!"

We do have a choice regarding our destiny. Heaven is there for the asking. Invite God into your life today. Ask Him to be your Lord and Savior. His free gift is yours for the asking. So go ahead . . . ask.

Live It!

If you wish to give your life to Jesus Christ, pray this simple prayer: "Dear God, I have sinned against you and am not able to pay for my sins. I know that Jesus died on His cross for my sins. I turn away from the way I was going and accept His payment on my behalf. I invite Him to be the Lord of my life from this day on. Amen."

Even though I walk through the

valley of the shadow of death,

I will fear no evil,

for you are with me;

your rod and your staff,

they comfort me.

—Psalm 23:4

PERSPECTIVE

How's your day going so far? Do you have some troubles following you around? Is something weighing you down today?

Listen to what British comedian Douglas Jerrold once said: "Troubles are like babies . . . they only grow by nursing."

Isn't that the truth? Our troubles are what they are. We often make them bigger than they need to be by dwelling on them until they begin to grow, at least in our minds.

God's Holy Bible asks, "If God is for us, who can be against us?" (Rom. 8:31). That positive outlook cuts our troubles down to proper size. When God is by my side as I walk through life, I feel much more confident about things that seem difficult to face. So today, why not trust your troubles to God? He will work with you to keep perspective while you meet what comes your way.

Live It!

When you are tempted to dwell on your problems, choose to focus on God and His provision instead. You'll enjoy the feeling!

And I try . . .

To touch the world like You

touched my life

And I'll find my way

To be Your hands

—Audio Adrenaline

KINDNESS

The movie *Pay it Forward* was about the random acts of kindness started by a young boy who had a simple dream to make the world a kinder place. He wanted to start a new world order where random acts of kindness would be passed from one person to another until the whole world became one big happy family. What a wonderful idea!

Let me suggest one simple adjustment to this noble idea: do your random acts of kindness with God in mind. When you do something on behalf of God, you imitate Him in a profound and wonderful way; you are human as you were truly meant to be.

Live It!

Let God touch your world through you, before this day is done. Change someone's life with a random act of kindness.

Ask and it will be given to you;

seek and you will find; knock

and the door will be opened to

you. For everyone who asks

receives; he who seeks finds; and

to him who knocks, the door

will be opened.

—Matthew 7:7–8

PROVISION

I like to begin each day by remembering some promise from God's Bible. Here's one for today: King David wrote: "I was young and now I am old, yet I have never seen the righteous forsaken or their children begging bread" (Ps. 37:25). When David was an old man, he looked back over his life and realized how faithfully God had cared for him.

God is still providing for people today. No matter what our circumstances are, if we have God in our lives and are willing to trust Him with everything, we can have confidence that He will meet our every need.

David was right. In spite of his inconsistent behavior and failures in life, God took care of him. Turn your life over to God, and one of these days you will be able to say "I have never seen the righteous forsaken, or their children begging bread."

Live It!

Do you have a nagging fear that you will be in want of something you need? Express that fear to God and ask Him for the faith to believe that His Word is true.

There is a time for everything, and

a season for every activity

under heaven. . . .

—Ecclesiastes 3:1

LEISURE

Bertrand Russell observed that one of the symptoms of an approaching nervous breakdown is the belief that one's work is terribly important. Many of us have bought into the lie that our work defines us. Even the best of people can fall into this trap if they're not careful and discerning.

This lie has ruined the lives of many families. Certainly, our jobs are important. Yet, for many of us, work has taken on a life of its own, becoming our master rather than our servant.

You may see that in the way your family has been acting lately. Tension and stress may have become the norm. Relationships that used to be healthy and wonderful may have become strained and distant.

If that describes your current existence, stop and take inventory of your life. On his deathbed, no one ever regrets not working more hours. But many will die with the regret of childhoods missed, relationships broken, and days filled with stress. Don't be one of them.

Live It!

Track your work hours this week. Compare them to the hours spent with family and friends. Make adjustments if necessary.

I have been crucified with Christ

and I no longer live, but Christ

lives in me.

—Galatians 2:20

UNSELFISHNESS

I heard about a CNN reporter traveling with the U.S. military in Iraq who offered his videophone to four marines so they could call their families. Rather than using the phone for himself, the first marine ran to get his sergeant, who hadn't spoken with his pregnant wife in three months. The reporter then offered the phone to the other three. They used the phone to call the parents of Lance Corporal Brian Buesing, who had been killed the week before. "Where do they get young men like this?" the reporter asked.

Jesus said, "Do to others what you would have them do to you" (Matt. 7:12), which we know as the Golden Rule. When those marines gave up their right to use the videophone for themselves and allowed others to go in their place, they experienced the pleasure of being used by God to help other people. In this world, my friend, it just doesn't get any better than that.

Live It!

If you find yourself waiting in a line today, let the person behind you go first, and do it with a smile!

Acknowledgements

I owe a debt of gratitude to—

Ron Heider, whose vision and passion served as the catalyst for our daily radio program.

Wendy Johnson, who assisted with the editing of these scripts.

The thousands of folk who make up Eastern Hills Wesleyan Church. I love you all. You're the best.

My church staff, especially Dan Scanlon, Mark Nigro, and Dawn VanDine, who serve with me daily in the Lord's work.

My wife and life's partner Anita; my son, Aaron; and my daughters, Bethany and Rachel. They mean the world to me and I love them dearly.

Jesus Christ, by (and for) whom I daily live and breathe.

KARL EASTLACK